YOU ARE NOT DEAD

CLEVELAND STATE UNIVERSITY POETRY CENTER
NEW POETRY

Michael Dumanis, Series Editor

For a complete listing of titles please visit
www.csuohio.edu/poetrycenter

YOU ARE NOT DEAD

Wendy Xu

Cleveland State University Poetry Center
Cleveland, Ohio

ISBN 978-0-9860257-0-9

First edition

17   16   15   14   13   5   4   3   2

This book is published by the Cleveland State University Poetry Center,
2121 Euclid Avenue, Cleveland, Ohio 44115-2214
www.csuohio.edu/poetrycenter and is distributed by
SPD / Small Press Distribution, Inc. www.spdbooks.org.

Cover image by Jelle Martens
You Are Not Dead was designed and typeset by Amy Freels in Garamond with
Helvetica Neue display.

LIBRARY OF CONGRESS CATALOGING-IN-PUBLICATION DATA
Xu, Wendy, 1987–
  [Poems. Selections]
You are not dead / Wendy Xu. — First edition.
    pages cm
Includes bibliographical references and index.
"Distributed by SPD / Small Press Distribution, Inc."—T.p. verso.
Poems.
ISBN 978-0-9860257-2-3 (paperback : acid-free paper)
I. Title.
PS3624.U7Y58 2013
811'.6—dc23
                    2012051266

Acknowledgments

Enormous thanks to the editors of the following journals where many of these poems first appeared, often in slightly different forms:

Banango Street
    "If You Feel That Living Is a Little Bit Sad"
    "Dear Future Where Everything Is Hypothetical Except for Joy"

Columbia Poetry Review
    "In June Like We Said But I Fell Out Of Love"

Connotation Press: An Online Artifact
    "Reasons Other People Go to the Theatre"
    "Unapologetic Poem"
    "Something Else Is Burning So You Don't Have To"

Dark Sky Magazine
    "If You Aren't Busy I Think I'm on Fire"

Diagram
    "You Think You Are Something Less Real Than You Are"
    "We Are Both Sure To Die" (Without coffee ...)
    "We Are Both Sure To Die" (Clutching a tiny ...)

Forklift, Ohio
    "Requirements for Seeing a Valley"

HOUSEFIRE
    "Like Whatever Makes You Not a Statue"

ILK
    "Tiny Palace"
    "The Future Doesn't Care About Your Breakfast"
    "Of Dream Where You Become a Suicidal Ceramic Fruit Bowl"
    "And Then It Was Less Bleak Because We Said So"

InDigest
    "You Are Not Who They Wanted You to Be"

Inter|rupture
    "It's Almost My Birthday Don't Tell Anyone"
    "Auditorium Poem"

Jellyfish
    "Several Altitudes of Not Talking"
NOÖ
    "We Are Both Sure to Die" (In a way the birds …)
Phantom Limb
    "The Total Number of Things That Matter Is On the Rise"
Red Lightbulbs
    "This Year I Mean to Be an Elephant"
    "Wow Is What I Want"
    "We Are Both Sure to Die" (With the morning …)
    "We Are Both Sure to Die" (And then the anonymous …)
Third Coast
    "Here in This New Place Is Your Memory"
Vinyl Poetry
    "Please Stand a While Longer in the Vast, Amazing Dark"
    "We Are Both Sure to Die" (During a football game …)
Whiskey Island
    "Is That a Country or Just a Place"
    "What It Means to Stay Here"
    "We Are Both Sure to Die" (In awe …)
    "We Are Both Sure to Die" (On moving day …)
    "We Are Both Sure to Die" (Later when everything …)

The poems "If You Aren't Busy I Think I'm on Fire" and "You Are Not Who They Wanted You to Be" also appeared in a chapbook *The Hero Poems* from H_NGM_N.

Two poems from the series "We Are Both Sure to Die" appeared as a pamphlet from Greying Ghost Press.

Thank you immeasurably: Michael Dumanis, Frank Giampietro, the Cleveland State University Poetry Center, and the Program for Poets & Writers at UMass-Amherst.

Thank you to my teachers and friends, especially Dara Wier, James Tate, Peter Gizzi, D. A. Powell, Nick Sturm, Leora Fridman, Ted Powers, Jeff Hipsher, Lech Harris, Kyle McCord, Matt Hart, Nate Pritts, and Jonathan Volk.

Thank you forever: Mom and Dad, Cindy, Spenser, Brodie, and Phil.

For my parents & for Cindy

Contents

3

4

5

6

Several Altitudes of
Not Talking

You are part of other people but not
like them. You live in a little wooden box
and wake up with your face
in your palm and some sunlight.
Which is a sign of resignation but not
for you. Which is part of what I meant
by trying to effect change
in myself and also talking. By describing
to you that before a city can become
spectacular its buildings must put on
an iron gown. And then some workers
climb all around it. And it is like having
no teeth because you are waiting
for better teeth. I tell you I am very attached
to my old teeth. In a game called *all of this
is hypothetical* I did not once slide
my teeth across the table. I do not
even remember what you offered
as the hypothetical exchange for a life
where I only drink soup. There were
some girls on their bikes
and wind. There were some people
reuniting after many years apart or just
a day. You were not like everyone else
making demands with wild
gesticulations. I thought about maybe
trying to sharpen my knowledge

of jokes. I thought about really needing a hug. A very important car with sirens rumbled by and sounded exactly right.

Is That a Country or
Just a Place

A well constructed fence is the best
thing in the known universe. Here comes
my horse. Here come my friends to help
me make the intimidating forest a stack
of sturdy logs. I am not saddled with any kind
of regret. I am not uncomfortable when
we talk about outer space. Here comes
one more thing that makes
us matter. We feed important documents
to a fire. We watch them curl up
and kiss. I am not curious about the number
of unknowable voids wheeling around
our solar system. We kick over
a barn and build it back. We push
a tractor to its limit. We are speeding away into
the trees now. We see the brilliant green
light spread out to hug us.

Here in This New Place
Is Your Memory

For P. Smith

Here in this new place it is reasonable to own
a dog or to tell somebody you've been needing
them less. A tree is always on a journey
toward becoming a better tree, limbs waving like eager sails
on an anchored ship. It is sad when you understand that nothing
else can come along. It is worse when you care
a little less. What you love requires a prioritized list, thus
that nothing is equal but to itself. And you are equal to a dangerous
ivory moon. Here there is sacrifice on the doorstep
of beauty. Here there is an altar made of sand. It dismantles
no less than itself to please the sea.

It's Almost My Birthday
Don't Tell Anyone

I go to sleep and wake up
different. You make a lengthy
drive across Iowa to find
the other end of Iowa, its fields
hung silent in iron sky. Claims
are always being made
about precision. If I were a bird
I would mean to be
the small kind. What is going on
in that room where
no one lives? It might fill
itself with delicate things,
some very nice iron bowls,
twelve miniature trees, all
of them aflame. How
many times did they tell you
you'd never make it? One day
is never longer than
the next, untangling film
from a canister. Somebody
means to measure you
by needle and light.
I take a quiet kind
of panic to the river.

What It Means to Stay Here

I lie in a bed and am away from all
my thoughts. I pledge all kinds of things
to the moon, how it speaks but not
to me. Giant land snail, you
are my friend. African prairie buck, you king
of going unseen, black horses moving
through the night. The wilds mean
many things and often we go on
into it. We put our precious bodies
in a tent. We have a lifespan and O how
we live it out. I don't know much
about anything. I drink my coffee and wait
for what is next. My fine house blows over
on a Tuesday and the anthem of what
this means is awfully sweet. Where
shall I wander before I finally
am gone? What do I bring back
in my careless hands to show you?

Reasons Other People
Go to the Theatre

Someone takes their private life and puts it
on a stage. And then it is still their life but other
people share it. It gets an opening night
and all the sidewalks are roped
in velvet. Famous people come
for the champagne. Regular people come
because it is Wednesday. Everybody wears
a hat that features a different bird depending
on how important they want to appear
at the reception. There is a brave pigeon circling
the nest of immaculate, white doves. Look
how one guy forgot his hat. Look
how a chandelier is more parts shine
than crystal. There are only sad reasons
for feeling sad and doesn't that seem right?
Look how the curtains have a purpose.
They have big red faces parted
by light. Look how they excel at hiding
the show from everything else.

You Are Not Who
They Wanted You to Be

But after years enough alone, even the wicked sleep.
Clematis in a window-box creeping the house, one thing overtakes
the next but is forgiven. I name everything in the sky
    Jupiter and you,
its moon claiming a synchronized orbit. No time for specifics,
    no proof
that we have ever met. Your irregular thought patterns are seen
by a doctor, but when the actual untelevised apocalypse
    comes I don't want
to be ready, a capsized tugboat blinking in the harbor
is how you'll know I stayed. No advantage now to buying in bulk.
The isolated incidents of suburban shovel crime in
    this neighborhood
mean it's OK to ask for help. Your courage changes the world.
    Your right hand
choking bottles like a songbird; sometimes hopelessness is a lie
feeding your sparrows to the dusk.

This Year I Mean to
Be an Elephant

I don't know if you understand me when
I say hopefully there is a future and we
are both allowed in it. I mean last year it
was OK just to be flattened by our ideas.
I sat in so many rooms and eventually felt
interesting and not like a chair. Do you
feel like a straight line? I worry about how
I don't. I worry that when I turn on
the radio this morning it sounds just like
I expect. I am thinking about kicking what
I expect in the shin. Last year I forgot
whole people until having lunch again
with those people. Last year I forgot really
embarrassing secrets like how I am allergic
to regular soap. Cue all the different kinds
of light and what music makes you feel
not dead. Last night I dreamt about sand.

Requirements for Seeing a Valley

For N. Sturm

You must be at least this tall. You must
not care that you are not. You need a friend who
is a plant scientist to point out all
the trees. This is a walking tour. Where
are your shoes? This is because airplanes will not
make stops in Ohio and I put that somewhere
in my letters. You must think that light watches
over you when everyone else
is talking. I put some sand in a jar and wait
for it to mean. Some horses wade into
the dangerous ocean because what else
is more important to see? Hold on, I promise
it's happening. You and me are something
like a forest.

Auditorium Poem

That the stars pull a wave toward
other coasts. That wolves are something
else until you meet one
in his own room. What was that story
about transgression? Wolves that lick
their gums and smile. Those same
stars I do not understand. The cold
has left me in it and the plants
are dead holding each other in the back seat
of a car. I didn't mean it. Sometimes
you have no choice but to drive
to Connecticut. I know my hands fold
on their own. I know falling
to my knees still means something.
That a basin of cool water still answers
the moon. Here you are. Here
you always have been.

Dear Future Where Everything Is Hypothetical Except for Joy

For T. Powers

Sitting here underground is the same
as sitting in a chairlift that spans several
mountains because I am paying attention.
If some girls come in wearing sashes then it is important
to be happy for other people. It is important
to celebrate girls that spend time decorating
each other's sashes because one girl is about
to love someone forever. If it is a little bit terrible
to tell someone that their hair or mannerisms
suit them especially well on a particular day. Look
how the sashes of the girls are swaying gracefully
beneath a traffic light. If a town is seriously
lacking in other places to go and so we stay
here. Someone is now speaking about how many candelabras
it takes to overwhelm a room. If here it seems
like a candelabra could be happy
its whole life. Look at how two pairs of tandem bikers
just went by and believably unplanned, how
important it could be to admit my life already
feels long and I will keep working
at the fulfilling. If in dreams there is no
question of who pulled whom from the lake
that was also for some reason burning, me
or the baby wolf. And if later I admit sheepishly
to Ted that too much of everything

seems recurring, it is acceptable to add more ice
to my terrible drink. I like to look
at people who sit there fascinated
by whatever they are talking about.
If later the streetlights shatter me
into pure amazement. Ted's glass
held up to them will somehow be swimming
with fire, but if it is supposed to be a surprise don't
ever tell me.

The Place Where I Live Is Different Because I Live There

On Friday all anybody did was talk
about waffles. When other people want
a thing I want it a lot too. Other people
wanted to save kittens from trees
while the trees maybe wanted
some saving also from the dark sort
of rain that fills a gutter. That shook out
some people from beds trying
to be happy. That caused a train full
of complicated ideas to stop near
my house which was great. I pay
attention to things that push
back. I muster up the energy to sit
through very important presentations.
One way to be amazed is to be
less amazing and then pay
attention. Don't ask any questions
about waffle science. Believe that there
was only ever one kitten whimpering
in the tree and how great
are you. Admire how things wait
to push up through
the earth until the earth
is beautiful enough. I think
about painting my house. Then
I think about other houses.

I Have Been Trying to Get Back
Some of That Old Feeling

Somebody says *What are you doing tomorrow!* and they
are outside my window. I am just driving
through snow with my friends wanting what
everyone wants. What if your face was a passionate treatise
on anything? I fell off a stupid bus into sound. It
was all blue and blue and blue. It was having enough
time to think nothing. Today we divide up animals
and climb inside. A defense against miniatures begins
I don't like to be relative.

Tiny Palace

Sorry that I ate all the best cubes
of watermelon. Picnics make me nervous
or hungry. There is a terrible cicada
thrashing about on the grass trapped
inside its own terrible shell. Its face
is a dark, vibrating marble. Things happen
but we get by. There's a dog
with a missing leg licking the face
of another dog. All of this takes place
inside a mysterious, tiny palace. You threaten
to tear it down. Build me a new one
in place of explaining why.

In June Like We Said
But I Fell Out of Love

Once I went to a costume party for the end
of the world where I was a meteor and my friend
a blue jay who scattered feathers all
over the room dancing. After she was just
a pale molted dress we sat there drinking
tequila on the roof and I was one year older.
She wore a mask for whatever reason covered in thousands
of tiny, blue crystals. My meteor dress had started to pull
apart at the craters. We talked about how everybody just wants
to be happy without ever really trying. She said *Yes, but
let's pretend we're different*, shaking a small fist at nothing
in particular. So we stayed up there in the dark for a while
thinking about what to think.

3

Like Whatever Makes
You Not a Statue

If you are an ocean then I think I am a music
video where everyone I know throws
a party. We wear those pointy hats and somehow
I feel gorgeous. Today I'll plant a tree knowing
it's fine without me. Today I'll climb into
a boat without any of my belongings. Do you
want to come too? Do you feel particularly
attached to what you make? I have dreams
about a ferris wheel rolling away from
its structural integrity. It goes on a gigantic tour
of North America unable or just unwilling
to stop. My mouth is a peach pit of everything
I've ever said. Everyone is laughing but only
you should know why.

Of Dreams Where You Become a Suicidal Ceramic Fruit Bowl

Sometimes you're throwing your body
from the cliffside as an apocalypse rumbles by
on a dozen white horses. The apocalypse has a sense
of humor and impeccable taste. It's unbelievable what
we demand from our loved ones. Easier to believe
that we're all just occupying an imaginary life
as dishware, cracked limbs whistling past each other
in the wind. It's almost melody. It's almost a tune your friend
hears in Kentucky, a clear note from an iron bell.
And really, who didn't have dreams
of being good last night? A truck hauled a carnival
across the desert. A bowl met some oranges
and you know the rest. Jeff still says there are wolves
beneath the window. They drag the city out
from under its bed sheet.

Wow Is What I Want

I know all about patterns and it goes my
brain then a triangulation of feelings then in
a different state you. In my past life I was just a math
equation and then I got promoted. Now I have
way more variables. Now I miss you and only
order carrots at lunch. You are a big stupid X
over everyone's mouth because everyone
is not speaking birds. I have been karate chopping
in my sleep. My sleep has been visited
by impossible wolves so much that I wake
up crying. I want to be some kind
of genuine. I would give you all my teeth for
the idea that you would want my teeth because
they are mine. In the first half of a day I think you
could be in movies. But I don't really love movies.

If You Find That Living
Is a Little Bit Sad

Someone's face framed by computer screen
is not the same as someone
in a room. Make choices, then watch
stuff happen. Say yes I agree to take up the dark
pail of my life before this one and empty
its guts into the river. The river thanks me
and shines harder. Overhead these indomitable
stars. This row of stern white houses
where I thought my friend lived, where
even now young people still gather
around a fire. The fire feels like being removed
from my own face. My own face turns toward
the shimmering water where it burns but
does not burn away.

The Total Number of Things
That Matter Is on the Rise

Someone right now is a nervous wreck, biking
against the dark ribbon of a highway like some kind

of quiet disaster. What is up with all these apartments
infested by bees? Why did you instead gently

ease the door back into its frame? How yesterday
a street magician produced a blossom of pennies

from his sleeve that impressed us all. Then a bird
he let go. Then a never ending ribbon flowing

to a single white rose which he tucked behind the ear
of a little girl. How often will you demand

silence before the reveal? If that sprawling road
never leads you to the sea, this hurricane

surely assembles worse on my doorstep. Someone
right now thinks to remove his slippers before hurrying

to the phone. Some terrible little bees dive
into your soup from the urgent rim.

You Think You Are Something Less Real Than You Are

You put on some new pants. I put
on some sunlight. I put on a coyote. You
put on a bigger coyote. You put on all
of the coyotes. You put on the sand as it flies
beneath your incredible little paws. I put on
rain not reaching the desert. You put on how we
feel sad after this. You put on the sadness. You
put on methods for dealing with it. The sadness tries
to put you on but you say *No!* You wrestle
the sadness to the ground. You are big and need
large wings. You put on the large wings. You are still
a coyote. You put on the howling. You put on
things that howl back. Nothing
you won't put on. You put on the darkness.
You put on some stars and also what
is between them. You put on the moon. The moon
that shines. You put on how we want
to stay here. You put on how we forget where
we were before. You put on the earth how
it cracks. You put on its face when it sees us.

And Then It Was Less Bleak
Because We Said So

Today there has been so much talk of things exploding
into other things, so much that we all become curious, that we
all run outside into the hot streets
and hug. Romance is a grotto of eager stones
anticipating light, or a girl whose teeth
you can always see. With more sparkle and pop
is the only way to live. Your confetti tongue explodes
into acid jazz. Small typewriters
that other people keep in their eyes
click away at all our farewell parties. It is hard
to pack for the rest of your life. Someone is always
eating cold cucumber noodles. Someone will drop by later
to help dismantle some furniture. A lot can go wrong
if you sleep or think, but the trees go on waving
their broken little hands.

We Need to Talk About Sarah

Sarah says we need to talk about Sarah. Sarah
is like *We need to talk, can we do that after this coffee?*
We need to talk about how Sarah
is always talking. The snow is always
snowing when we talk about a way
to move our mouths. Sarah and I finish
each other's lunch. Sarah and I are like *What
is a way to move slower?* I say *Sarah, what if you
are a ghost?* Sarah makes a face like she
is telling me something about French fries
and staying awake. I say *Sarah, let's think about people
we might have missed.* Sarah says we need to talk
about going missing.

Please Stand a While Longer in the Vast Amazing Dark

Maybe don't for another minute be afraid
of anything. Because swimming is really useful
against drowning which you didn't know until
you tried it. And then your life was just massive
regret. And then you thought about three
purple blossoms in the hair
of a beautiful girl. But that's not the part
that aches in a deep kind of place
inside you. Like if your dinner caught fire
in your stomach and then you ran
to the river which was dry. And your friend
was a jerk who didn't share resources
including a hose. Most things lose
interest when you are quiet
and small. Most things want to be
around other majestic things that make
noise or beauty. Wind plucks a flower
for sailing. You stand there in the presence
of whatever you are not.

4

From Inside the Machine
It Is Not a Machine

From inside I am just a blur with
some buttons for a face. I am not
a pointy snowflake blowing around
over the perfect river. The machine says *How
did you get here and why are you
not loud?* I lie down in all
of this mud. I can talk to anyone
I want including when someone
is a pancake. Someone is the lid
to tupperware I go back and rescue.
That is the part the machine
says it almost likes.

Unapologetic Poem

For E. White

There are reasons to ride a bike not
related to joy. But you don't believe in not
believing. I believe in blaming everything
on the highway, big dumb highway sliding
toward conclusions. One of you and one
of me, to be numerous. We handle
ourselves like some kind of gospel. I go
for a walk to tell you about this terrible
dream involving wolves. You and I
went down into the cave. We went down
like we knew what we were doing. We
went down and it mattered. Everything
matters when you are reverently displaced.
But you don't say anything
about moving through all those stars.

If You Aren't Busy I Think I'm on Fire

I worry that someone is right about the end of the world.
If we performed an elaborate ritual
to prevent it, who could say we didn't succeed? The deer live
on to cause another traffic jam, white tails flaring
in the sun. There is no way to disprove
you are infinite. I walk into a yellow house and a calendar
says 1973, the ceilings drag wires from room
to empty room. If we ordered the total annihilation of other people,
would we still need other people? Sunlight coming down
like a yellow tambourine of leaves.

If It Turns Out You
Forget to Say Anything

It is the best thing that has ever happened. It is like
throwing a golden monkey wrench
down a hallway. Like seven horses suspended
over the ocean by stars as you look up
from your boat because sailing is about
possibilities. What happens to what we say now belongs
to no one. I think what is important is going
to the shore and staying awhile. Everyone
is dying from loneliness. Everyone flees
from inside the forgotten zoo.

Poem for Inappropriate Caring

Every morning a baby cries somewhere down
the street. It is not actually on the street it
is in a house with an open window somewhere
down the street. *I don't care* is what
I always say. Sometimes I say *I don't care* followed
by *Whatever* followed by picking up
an apple and eating it in a way that looks
like *Shut up.* You chipped a tooth eating
mixed nuts and I was like *I don't care.* I had
a cat and lost it which was worth even
less caring. My foot meets an iron rail. My face
doesn't see other faces but I am all like seriously
I don't care. My face waits for when
I am dreaming or dead.

5

Something Else Is Burning
So You Don't Have To

The Yacht Club caught fire but you
were not there, you were wearing
a purple hat and all your hair flying
around under it. There are no rules
about looking great while other
people panic. Wind contributed
to this but mostly the fire. I feel bad
about waking up in the morning
and not thanking God that I
am not a match. Usually I drink
some coffee and continue being
a person. Sometimes you leave
and the cactus grows away
from itself. Sometimes you move
to Japan and come back
in a year. I stay in a fabulous
apartment without you. Every time
a person rings my doorbell it plays
a new tune. When the measure
of music floats to my bedroom
it is always an unfamiliar kind
of knowing.

Things Other People Are Good At

There was a unicorn
in the movie and it
had lost its horn
so it was actually
just not a horse.

—

A lot of things
happen and then
I forget. And
the things
I forget belong
to the cold earth.
When I dig
them back up
they are not
the same.

—

The only thing
I ever made
which is worth
anything
at all
is a promise
to my friends
to keep
moving.

—

Yes I like
football because
everyone is on
a team.
Teams are people
who tell you
when you're
doing it all
wrong.

—

Loving someone
once is really
terrible because
then you know
it's great
and the opposite
of losing
your keys.

—

I tried to be
serious about
getting older but
getting older
was so funny
because you get
stuff you know
you have to
return but
you act like
you don't and
hang on
desperately until
you forget
what you had
in the first place
before all of this
stupid
trying.

—

On the Way to Connecticut
We Admire Its Absurdity

For J. Volk

Tell me when you decided to stop asking
for my advice all together. All together I come up
with nothing to tell you. Let's pull into this KFC
for biscuits. We missed all the parties buried
in amazing buckets of snow. We didn't miss
the snow until it left us. You had a little bit
of courage left to give me, and I am using it all to get
to Connecticut when the wet sprawl
of an interstate demands too much. Everything laid
out like a question. I have a question.
There are limits to how much we care
about other people. Other people don't
know or mean to think it.

If It Is Still Unclear What Kindness Means to Me

In the morning tandem bikers laugh
from one end of the street to the other, the children
holding fast to their fathers. Look at everyone how
they are happy. The birds skitter over
with gift worms writhing in their mouths.
There are many trees covered entirely by moss
like miles of terrible compasses. You remark gently
Not everyone can be your kind, so go on living
your life like you promised already.

We Are Both Sure to Die

Without coffee and only minor explosions
to spell our names. A bird
meeting a clear pane of glass. Fanfare
and various stems of wine. People circulating
in a slow, meaningful fashion around
others exchanging gifts. One time you
gave me a gift. One time everything
was rare and dispensed in intricate
packaging. One time it was a real accomplishment
to find you a coat to wear
into a mountain and its forgiving silence.
But I wore a coat into the mountain
and heard all kinds of secret mountain chatter.
One time there were no souvenirs
I could bring you. An example
of you forgiving me is you still making
a movie about my life. Where I am played
by someone better looking. Give her some lines
of quiet but spectacular regret.

We Are Both Sure to Die

Later when everything is
like a surface. How it all
collects light is an incredibly easy
place to invest our faith. Ok
but where did you go? Why aren't
we sharing something nice
or expensive? Everywhere
miniature airplanes, everywhere
more wings! Things to tell
time to tell you about death.
Not about when your body
is over. But about
death which is something impossibly
far away. We are not dead.
We still adventure in a completely
original way. Just coconut or
wearing stripes for dinner.
Good weather or hello.
I have been waiting forever
to meet you with all these books.
The sky no longer angry.
How does it feel now
with your head still stuck
inside the amazing sun?

We Are Both Sure to Die

Before an absolutely crucial conversation
about surfaces. Like *Hello I think I am the lid
to this candy dish,* my body full up
with light and usefulness. What if I just want
to dance? What if I believe in some kinds
of smashing? I don't mean
to throw myself from any high point
or sacred mountain. What if I am just
a malformed candle? What if you
are a riddle? What if I am on fire and I
like it? Where did you hear that thing
I forgot?

We Are Both Sure to Die

With the morning like a sledgehammer and that
is exciting. The morning. The sledgehammer is just
a bad joke. I tell you so many bad jokes. I feel
ashamed when people with outstanding
personalities walk by and show off fifteen different ways
of talking about amazement. The fifteenth is skiing. You
have never been anywhere with snow. You bought
a gigantic house not in a valley. We eat snacks
and drink exotic teas inside. We are moving now.
In space but also time. We are running out
of time. I find a single white tree in the forest. It
is dead but also waiting for color. Nothing is actually
wrong with anything ever. The sky opens up like
it is happy to see us. Here comes
some beauty. Eager and broken light.

We Are Both Sure to Die

On moving day throwing boxes
down the stairs. You throw a box
at my face. It blooms like a tiny
pink flower. Oh shit, we forgot all
the other boxes. Nobody else agreed
to help us move. The house
we are moving to is under the ocean.
You can't swim. I hate swimming.
You say *Whatever, swimming
is stupid.* We are not complicated
animals. We only need this one lamp.
We pack it all into the car.
The car is not invited.

We Are Both Sure to Die

And then the anonymous bouquet
of peonies arrives making room
for a little kindness before
everything starts to smolder in
an attractive way. I feel a sort of awful
regret about animals I have never
seen in real life. Worse, do you worry
you'll stop caring? My friends glue
ponies to the dashboard and we go
for a ride. We stare off into space for long
periods of time to mean please God let
us be real! I am here and love
to tell you. I am wearing that feeling
of being wrong like an old scarf.
Please tell me and tell me and tell
me about the river. Tell me what
birds mean to keep it.

We Are Both Sure to Die

In a way the birds find less
than compelling. I build a nest and grow
better feathers. I was sailing in a ship that came across
another ship in an ocean humbled
by sunlight. Kissing is like steering
with purpose. But kissing is also like confusion
at the supermarket if you really love
the supermarket. Which I do. Which why
do we eat birds? Which when you have
a birthday why do you tell me? Everything
I said yesterday was a lie. I don't love any city
better than the next, except when you are a city
grown tired of senseless conflict
which is broadcast on the evening news.
Then I am terribly aware of being just one
person with a body. Then I draw up quietly
some charts and at the very top misspell
your honest name.

We Are Both Sure to Die

In awe of what we forgot
to do. Now the stove is on fire
and the fridge is on fire and you
are haunted by what you
remember. *It is OK* I tell you and motion
to what's beyond the window.

We Are Both Sure to Die

Clutching a molten piece of someone
else's life. I tried sleeping
in this bed of heavy light. I tried moving
out into the forest and failed at touching
a deer. Say you will be nothing or
beside me. How best do we correspond
in the darkness of a year? But look the year
rolls over and has given me a new face. Now
you go toward the ocean with that terrible
spirit of discovery. There is getting to know
your body and disowning it. The ocean says you
are not dead. What else do you want
it to announce?

We Are Both Sure to Die

But I feel like a person again. I feel
like more than enough snow
to cover a bicycle. I feel like what
is in the snow. I feel like what
says yes to snow. I feel like what
is before snow. What is before
snow? I feel like an interesting kind
of tired, like a wind chime
at night. I feel like a porch that
is also a wind chime. I feel a little
fine. I feel like talking not
on the phone. I feel like
the phone. I feel like you are something
I say in the dark. I feel like what
is an airplane in summer.

We Are Both Sure to Die

During a football game so consider
there will be other people. But they
can't come with us. But they can't know
that the most amazing part of waking up
is you are not dead. You are wearing
a totally splendid bathrobe that hugs
you like a dress. Hopefully there is some
coffee for how I am tired. Hopefully my head
opens up like a rose.